me? can you see me? can you

ou know me? can you see me? can you hear me?

me? do you know me? can you see me? can you

ou hear me? do you know me? can you see me?

e? can you hear me? do you know me? can you

ou see me? can you hear me? do you know me?

me? can you see me? can you hear me? do you

ou know me? can you see me? can you hear me?

me? do you know me? can you see me? can you

ou hear me? do you know me? can you see me?

e? can you hear me? do you know me? can you

ou see me? can you hear me? do you know me?

me? can you see me? can you hear me? do you

u know me? can you hear me? do you know me?

MW01680099

This book is a tribute to the inspiring work
of Mutual Ground, Inc.
and other organizations and individuals
who also work to nurture, empower,
and enrich the lives of others.

CAN YOU SEE ME?

An Unveiling of the Human Spirit

Wishing you a world filled
with bold beauty,
hope and truth.

TO

FROM

Images contained herein are for illustrative purposes only
and are not intended to depict any actual event or circumstance.

Front cover: DARKNESS IN LIGHT... *and still we dream*, Oil on canvas, 30 x 24 inches
Page 3: detail of photo of Karen Holt and Gene Wilson
Page 6: detail, portrait in oil of Bronwyn Ashley Cole, Lawrence J. Pelka, Kelly Nicastro, Heather Lowell, Bess Kindlon, Elaine Schneider
Page 7: detail, portrait in oil of Brett Ashley Hood, Amber Achilles, Owen Nicholas Sawyer

Copyright © 2001 Karen Holt
Photographs Copyright Karen Holt Classical Art & Portraiture
Foreword Copyright © 2001 by Marilyn Van Derbur

All rights reserved. No part of the content of this book may be reproduced or transmitted in any form or by any means, electronically or mechanically, including photocopying, recording, or by any information storage and retrieval system, without permission in writing from the author.

Published in 2001 by

CHIARO PUBLISHING / Dallas, Texas
PMB 119, 18484 Preston Road
Suite 102, Dallas, TX 75252

ronisaacson@earthlink.net

Substantial discounts on bulk quantities of this book are available to corporations, professional associations and other organizations. For details contact Chiaro Publishing.

Publisher's Cataloging-in-Publication
(Provided by Quality Books, Inc.)

Holt, Karen, 1946 -
Can you see me? : an unveiling of the human spirit / by Karen Holt ; foreword by Marilyn Van Derbur ; design by Tina Cauller. -- 1st ed.
p. cm.
ISBN 0-9712005-4-8

1. Holt, Karen, 1946- 2. Holt, Karen, 1946 - -- Themes, motives.
3. Hope in art. 4. Self-acceptance -- Poetry. 5. Healing in art.
6. Art therapy. I. Title.

ND237.H675A4 2002 759.13
QBI01-700901

DESIGN: Tina Cauller
PRODUCTION COORDINATION: Steven Goff / Erik Ko

Printed in China through Palace Press International, San Francisco, CA

10 9 8 7 6 5 4 3 2 1
FIRST EDITION

In memory of my twin brother,
Gene Allen Wilson,
and his undying song of spirit and courage.

Editor's Note

"Human beings respond to chiaroscuro as a thing of beauty, sensing balance and completeness."

— Grant Williams, Professor Emeritus
Vocal consultant to the Dallas Symphony Chorus

There is a word used often in the field of music and visual art — *chiaroscuro*. It is derived from two Italian words; *chiaro*, meaning light and clearness, and *scuro*, meaning dark and obscure.

As a part of music, it brings dimension to the feeling embodied within the musical work; *chiaro* — the overtones or brightness of timbre created while singing, *scuro* — the hollow, resonating sound that brings body and fullness to the voice.

Chiaroscuro is also a component of the visual arts, describing the relationship of light and darkness as integral to the creation of a good painting.

Without this relative balance, there is no shape discernable to the eye. It is the combination of the two elements, light and darkness, chiaroscuro, that defines the image.

Art, whether music or a painting, contains and emotes expressive feeling with the inclusion of chiaroscuro, the relativity of light with darkness, clearness with obscurity. And so it is with life.

Without darkness, there is no recognition of the light; there is no awareness of light without the darkness. Without an understanding of the obscure or hidden, there is no clarity. One is only discovered after the experiencing of the other. The overlay of these two intrinsic qualities, lightness and darkness, create chiaroscuro, bringing artistry into our lives.

Karen's paintings possess this chiaroscuro; walk into her work, and you will also.

— Ron Isaacson

Wishing you
creative joy,
wild purpose, and
love,
Karen Holt
2011

CAN YOU SEE ME?

An Unveiling of the Human Spirit

KAREN HOLT

Foreword by Marilyn Van Derbur

DESIGN BY TINA CAULLER

CHIARO PUBLISHING / DALLAS

Contents

Foreword

BY MARILYN VAN DERBUR
Former Miss America, named "Outstanding Woman Speaker in America",
Founder of SUN, an adult survivor program

Motivational speaking has been my full time career since I was in my early twenties. I never felt at a loss for words.

Then in 1991, my worst nightmare came true. A newspaper woman took my story of incest to the front pages. It stayed on the front pages for three days. My eldest sister, Gwen, then came forward as an incest survivor.

I was running from the press, from the story. Until, later that morning, in an effort to 'get away from it,' my husband, my daughter and I went to the high school track to jog.

A woman who was there often with her two dogs stopped me. "We are so proud of you, Marilyn. And I'm so grateful Gwen came forward this morning."

"Really, why?"

"Because yesterday, on our most popular radio talk show, people were calling in and saying, 'why should we believe her?' Now that your sister has come forward, they will have to believe you."

I was stunned. For thirty years, I had been one of the outstanding women in Colorado. I looked at her and said, "If people won't believe 53-year old me, then who, dear God, will believe a *child*?"

Like iron filings to a magnet, the entire picture went together for me, and that day became the first day of the rest of my life.
I began speaking about the unspeakable.
But there have been so many times when
I could not find the words to express the shame
I felt or the ugliness I felt or the isolation I felt.
Where are the words?

I found the expression of some of those feelings in Karen Holt's powerful paintings. I *know* what the woman is feeling in her painting DARKNESS IN LIGHT... *and still we dream.* And she knows what I have felt. There are no words. I can *feel* her pain, her isolation, her despair.

But Karen goes far beyond that. She goes full circle by giving us hope — through her painting, I AM ME AND YOU ARE YOU, we see children in all of their innocence and we know we must make this a safer world for these children.

Karen is a gifted artist who has experienced the highs and the lows of life. Just as the low notes give the fullness to a concerto, Karen uses all of the colors and feelings to allow us to experience our own memories and our own hopes for the future.

Begin Karen's book and you won't put it down. Finish her book and you won't forget it. Karen's paintings and words are a gift to all.

— MARILYN VAN DERBUR

Introduction

I carry wounds in my heart.
I paint to heal.
I paint to face my fears.
I paint so that I can hear my own voice.
I am painting to be heard.
I am painting so that other voices can be heard.

Together, soft voices become as thunder.

— Karen Holt

If we are each of immense value and worthy of being loved, then even I, must be. And, as I accept this basic truth, I must also accept my simple and seemingly insignificant story as significant. I share this chapter in my life for those who now feel as I have felt, and are searching for more — much more.

My book is a journal of how artistic expression permeates the walls of secrecy, revealing the real, and restoring the dignity of self. It documents, over a 20-year span of time, the transformative power of creativity, a conduit to that Higher Power greater than ourselves, that source of light and life which I call God. It expresses a chapter in a woman's life that has been lifted up from a suffocating darkness. My twin brother and I were robbed of our dignity and a part of ourselves as children through the abusive and unpredictable hands of an alcoholic father. The death and the life of my brother have led me into the world of art, and in so doing, into the knowing of me.

Paintings are the inside of the artist revealed; they are intimate portraits of the expressive being. They document the living and relentless human spirit, that part of us which transforms and transcends us beyond the base, into our human possibilities.

When our creativity is fearlessly and honestly accepted into our being, we are offered a direct link and language to the whisperings of our soul. The rumbling of life becomes audible. The reality of ourselves and of God becomes visible.

CAN YOU SEE ME? An Unveiling of the Human Spirit is a collection of the whisperings of my soul, where images and words emerged upon the canvas, and I unknowingly began to release my voice. The paintings and poetry speak through the silence — in spite of the silence.

This book offers each of us a way to know ourselves and others better. It encourages us to find the strength to walk into the fray of barking dogs — to stay on our own personal, true north heading. It is about listening, and it is about seeing; the spotlight is on us.

Without the courage to see, the human spirit is not visible. Courage is its leader; all other virtues follow. Love, hope, compassion, dignity — each are sustained and led by courage.

This book represents a step of courage for me as a human being. It is my sincerest and deepest hope that we each find the strength and courage — to see.

— Karen Holt

CAN YOU SEE ME?

An Unveiling of the Human Spirit

Paintings & Poetry

by Karen Holt

I AM ME & YOU ARE YOU

… breathe, balance, stretch — find your melody

Yes, we are all loved. Let's celebrate!
Stand up. Jump.
Pat your head and rub your stomach.
Sing zip-a-dee-doo-dah and twirl around.
Balance on one foot and then the other.
Open your heart and let your melody spill out.
Celebrate you and celebrate me,
and celebrate the Love that walks with us,

Joining our hearts.

u know me? can you see me?

Looking Directly
...into the ebe eyes of life

Survival is the preface for a life
vibrating with rich potential.

To survive is to be offered the opportunity to inspire.
The true measure of our strength
is determined not by the instinctual act of surviving,
but by the acceptance of the gift of all gifts — life.

We then begin moving towards
the opening door that awaits
the strongest of hearts,
those ready to breathe, speak,
and live with passion.

We can now drop the clothing
of the survivor — it is without
texture, color or vibrancy.
It is a temporary wrap,
one that protects, but also removes
and isolates — one that closes the heart
and numbs the soul — one never designed to be worn forever.

For when we find that pulsating strength
of the spirit, the gift from
the greatest of Givers — we begin!
We rise,
trembling with bold purpose,
vulnerable to all that is offered,

Looking directly... into the eyes of life.

o you know me? can you see me?

survival

is

the

preface

for

a

life

vibrating

with

rich

potential

FORGIVING... *invites love*

Unveiling

The redness of rage slashes open my walls,
and buried emotions tumble onto the canvas.
Jagged fears, entrapment and despair look back,
each once, a part of me.

The healing power of color and canvas become evident in this self-awareness exercise of three paintings: *Rage Released*, *Swirls of Springtime* and *Eyes of a Child*, all created within a 30-minute period. Emotions are painted, felt and then released — no thinking, no self-editing, no masterpiece here. Simple, spontaneous, and sincere feelings surface, when we give ourselves permission to explore.

Releasing

Petals open and naturally fall away,
dancing sunshine spills over the cloth,
laced with swirls of warm springtime hope.
Quiet calm awaits.

Seeing

A hidden part of myself moves forward,
a part that would not die.
She is revealed, unearthed from darkness.
A child emerges with unfamiliar brushwork.
Eyes filled with sadness, look into mine,
as we see one another for the first time.
She has survived, endured alone, and waited always.

Accepting

Through tears, forgiveness invites love,
and we are wrapped as one.
I have found wholeness.
We are complete.

d o   y o u   k n o w   m e ?   c a n   y o u   s e e   m e ?

A Rose is a Rose is a Rose

... within

To believe in yourself, when few others do,
  with eyes that see the truth, even in the darkest of moments,
to walk away, parched by tears of pain, towards your own vision,
  singularly strong, guided by the answers burning in you,
is to begin.

Moving on, preserving the heart so that it can love,
  clearing a space to blossom, we climb, soaking in the warmth,
storing it away, remembering —
  blowing away the seeds of distrust.

Unfolding into a caring wisp of grace —
  reaching out to not only be held, but to hold,
the hand that was empty, now cradles the delicate petals.
  Smiles of the heart are shared.
Flowers of the soul, blossom.
  For, within, a rose is a rose, is a rose, is a... rose.

Originally painted in 1989, repainted in 1997 — same subject, same canvas, same artist, but a dramatic transition within the artist is clearly evident. Pain and numbing coldness fill the first, serenity and warmth move her brush in the second painting.

do you know me? can you see m

Darkness in Light

. . . and still we dream

Her stillness seems unaffected by time.
And yet, I hear a screaming urgency, for her needs cry out for more.

She needs to feel understood.
She needs someone to listen.
She needs a place to be, a reason to be there, a reason to be.
She needs to feel the life-giving effects of

love.

She needs me, she needs you, she needs us,
and
we need her!

For it is she who will be most affecting in touching another desperate soul…

for
she
deeply
understands.

DECUMANO
INFERIORE
USCITA
you know me? can you see me?

THE POTTER... *and the clay*

We are as holding vessels,
We not only contain, but we
carry,
convey,
and circulate that which we are holding.

A gentle touch nudges, reshapes, and refines,
while our hearts are held in the sculptor's hands.

As we move out of the darkened corners of
existence
and into the heat of life,
we connect and fuse with others,
becoming a conduit of sharing.

We are hollow, so that we can be filled.
And we are filled, so that we may share.
Love shapes the pots and fills their emptiness.

Love does overflow.

o you know me? can you see me?

can you see me? can you hear me?

Coming Back

... greeting yesterday today

Decorated with spider webs and dust, on a darkened basement floor,
sits a trunk holding memories,
carefully stored, long before today.

But, we are fragile no more.
Today the locked lid is flung open,
as the memories are scooped out, shattering the depths of self,
different, oh so different from those floating earlier in the air.

With acceptance of the truths, surges of renewed strength fill the soul.
A solitary journey back, ultimately moves us forward.
As eyes turn towards tomorrow,
Greeting yesterday, today.

can you see me? can you hear me

Inseparable Companions

… my shadow & I

Casting shadows of shape,
sunlight paints mirrored curves of color.

Repeating patterns, mimic life's tangibles,
attempting to replicate,
stepping in rhythm with its leader.

Created by light touching form,
it glances over and off,
leaving its imperfect imitation
strewn across the stone-laden paths of time.

As sunshine spills upon us,
swirls of life are sampled together,
Inseparable companions – my shadow and I.

Tomorrow…

o you know me? can you see me?
KAREN HOLT

THE HEALING OF A HEART

Art offers us a chance to see into ourselves. The painting or writing pulls you, creates a pause, draws you forward. When we step into the painting, we step through the walls, see through the veils, feel the buried emotions — we listen to our hearts. And through that connection — healing begins.

We each have held pain, sorrow, despair — deeply inside. We have placed them in a darkened cell; the key has been misplaced. Art can help you find the key. It initiates the desire to search for that key. Sometimes, it is the key. Art can be the translation of, or the interpretation of another heart — it can be the impetus in finding our own.

When the creative spirit expresses the innermost depths of an artist, the art will speak to another at that same level. It will stir, bother, take or move us into our own odyssey or voyage, into our own heart. It will break open that brittle shell and nourish, warm and hold gently.

We will become a part of the music, the painting, or the play, and ultimately life, and through this connection, art begins the healing.

It is all about stepping into and becoming a part of our own story — pausing to see, to feel, to know ourselves. We begin to acknowledge we are not alone with these feelings, this part that cried to be hidden, and at the same time, to be heard. There is hope in the knowing.

Veiled emotions move forward. They are recognized. They are acknowledged as a part of humanity. They are pulled out and examined and felt and honestly viewed. Then, they are replaced and moved to the background, and the fear of knowing loosens its hold. Our emotions pulsate, becoming an integral part of an integrated life.

Through my paintings, I am passing on to others a part of me, a part of my heart. And in the giving, I experience healing. Art sings, when it contains the colors and the brushwork of the heart.

A Boat

... that will carry two

Quietly
  unexpectedly
    a song floats through my heart
a song that feels warm, like a cupped hand that gently holds, not only me.
Easing me through the waters —
  singing:

"You are not alone here.
I have always been here for you, and I will always be.
I have given you a way to move through these waters stretching before you.
Step into this boat, and when you do, look around —
  and then invite another to join you.
Reach out your hand, and help them in.
Open your heart, and give it to that person.
Together, row the boat.
Together, move through the water."

For love is gentle and kind,
  and
    there is a boat that will carry two.

Life Before You

… each a part of the symphony

The hearts of those past and those before us,
create a stream of oneness,
flowing, moving, ever-changing,
just as salty waves wash in,
and then,
out.
We are each a member of this family.

We stand today, our vision limited, unable to see the beginning or the end.
Life's lived, and to be lived,
an intermingling of hearts shared,
hellos and farewells are bid, seemingly, in the same breath,
as the incessant steps of life rush forward.

We celebrate this gathering of hearts.
Food and music overflow.
The connection remains — then, and now.
Life's past and present survive to pass on the cup to future kindred souls.
Wisdom will be garnered along the way.

Drink deeply now, so that it may be shared
with the symphony of life before you.

can you see me? can you hear me?

o you know me? can you see me?

you see me? can you hear me?

When truth is locked away, we live in a cold box — no exits, no entrances. But as we unearth the secrets of our hearts, the world begins to glow with fresh air, sunshine and life. The same canvas is painted three years later, following the discovery and acceptance of the artist's inner truth.

Awakening

A new day is born
only after the shadowy night
has come to an end.

Within the night's darkness,
secrets may be hidden,
reality camouflaged,
ugliness may be blocked from our consciousness.

But with the illumination of a new day
comes an awareness,
a sharpening of the senses,
and a cleansing warmth moves through our being.

Love is felt
and the courage to know ourselves is found.

Awakening…

KAREN HOLT

A Place to Be

... where fear falls away

The rippling reflection mirrors the truth.
Looking into it deeply, I can no longer turn
away.
The past rushes forward, only to move away again
yet never disappearing, forever a part of me.

My heart cries out for those things I cannot
undo.

Comforting arms of acceptance wrap around
and
fears begin to gently, quietly — fall away.

Peace is mine,
for I have painted a place to be.

c a n   y o u   s e e   m e ?   c a n   y o u   h e a

Banjo Break

… the strings are to be strung, the song to be sung

"Banjo Break" is a painting of a song,

a song of celebration — of life past and present,

a song of joy,

a song of humanity in harmony,

a song of voices coming together,

and a song with rhythm and brightness and warmth.

Neither of the musicians depicted in *Banjo Break* is my brother, Gene. But they clearly represent his love of life — two creative musicians, coming together to share the moment, the spirit and the song. Isn't that what art and living are all about? Gene was not famous, or well-recognized, but he affected and changed lives.

At age 33, Gene was a real estate broker, had a girlfriend, a dog named Wolf, played volleyball and biked, and he loved to sing and make music with his friends. He had been doing so since he was a small child. He was a self-taught, sensitive, and masterful musician, with a clear, tenor voice, often singing along with his instrument of choice — the guitar, piano, or the banjo. He wrote songs, he sang songs, he played songs… and he listened to songs. He offered a bit of himself to each of us.

Gene was one of my best friends. Gene was also my twin brother.

He entered a UCLA Intensive Care Unit with encephalitis and then later, was transferred to a rehabilitation hospital. He struggled for nine months to live. In spite of their combined efforts, he was not rehabilitated, and he did not survive. But his song has survived, and therein lies our hope.

The shadows on the wall dance in memory of those who sang before us; I think of Gene. The banjo on the windowsill lies resting but for a moment. It will be picked up again.

For you and I have our own song to sing… *together*.

A tribute to my twin brother, Gene, who never stopped singing...

— Karen Holt

c a n   y o u   s e e   m e ?   c a n   y o u   h e a r   m e

With Me

... like the music of the heart

With me,
twin-like togetherness,
not carbon copies,
no duplications of the soul,
but an identity inexplicably linked.

From all known beginnings, we have breathed together.
Until the sun falls into quietness,
even then
and even now.

Like music of an ever-tumbling brook,
flowing, sliding, washing over and through,
creating its own path,
you find your way to me,
and
rest
inside
my
heart.

My twin,
the one who is always...
with me.

can you see me? can you hear me?

Daybreak

… dancing with light

As the morning crests the horizon,
revealing the sandy, crystalline dance floor of the sea,
the emergent star spreads satin threads of light over all.
Luminescent sunbeams glaze with brushstrokes of glowing warmth.
It skids over the caps of the rippling, rhythmic sea.
It lightens the cloud-strewn sky.
It caressingly rests upon a shoulder,
or a turned cheek.
It touches our eyes, sparkling, reflecting hope.
It strengthens,
giving us permission to play, to risk, to move anew, and to absorb.
It awakens our captured, sleeping spirit
and frees it to fly,
twirling with joy,
pausing to know peace,
reaching, beginning to understand,
our visions stretch forward.
Dancing with the dawn, our unspoken dreams mesh with reality.

In fluid movement, daybreak unfolds into morning.
And we move from darkness…
into light.

o you know me? can you see me?

Barefoot Youth

... unraveling, reflecting, and rephrasing

Stop writing my script.
Stop defining normal and then notice that I am not.
Stop defining life's values and then hoping I will live within.

This is me.
Let me be me.
I am one of many,
but, I am the one I am, and not
like any of the many.

I am Me!

o you know me? can you see me?

can you see me? can you hear me

Chrysalis... *it is time*

Wake up.
Open your star-dusted eyelids.
Let the sparkle of light flutter inside.
The sun is soaring upward.
An invitation to join the dance is hallelujahed
across the sky.

A new day is emerging.
It is the springtime of your life.

A melody pulls at your wings.

Let's fly.

Feeling permeates the same lovely face in both paintings, expressing the often diverse and multi-layered colors of the heart. Look into *Emerald* and see veiled coolness, untouched mystery. Then turn toward *Chrysalis* and find brightness emerging, a face that is alive, expansive and renewed. Color speaks.

s e e   m e ?   c a n   y o u   h e a r   m e

HOME IS… *in a child's heart*

Home is
  warm,
    light, and
      full of air.

It is a place where I can be alone and still feel safe.

Home means freedom to skip,
  slide in my socks,
    climb to the top of the flagpole,
      or give my teddy bear a hug.

Home is where I can learn to do it all by myself and — feel really good.

Home is where I sometimes hear no, instead of yes,
  where real and imaginary are both wonderful, but very different.

Home is where someone loves me,
where someone hears me — and,

where someone will answer.

PASSED

. . . from father to son

Relax.
Take slow breaths and listen.

Heartbeats fill the air.
The steps of life tread silently.

Rooms are filled with stories,
remembered and forgotten.

Peals of music-filled laughter bounce lightly through the halls.
as salty tear-like droplets slide down inside my heart.

And yesterdays bubble up before my eyes,
swirling,
dancing,
disappearing.

A heritage, a legacy, a life, a poem…
Passed
from father to son.

o you know me? can you see me?
Karen Hoys 1996 ©

Flowers Bend

... toward the sun

Just when the path looks clear,
  it becomes twisted.

As soon as I know the way,
  there is another.

The sun predictably rises and sets, but it illuminates
  the ever-changing, ever-moving,
    the soon-to-be discovered hopes of tomorrow,
      the dreams of today that lie dormant.

The fertile vastness and rich unpredictability of life spreads before us —
blossoming,
  the child unfolds its petals one by one,
    stretching closer to the potential of its own individual fullness and immensity.

Dreams reach out and gently nudge the heart, and we step onto the path again and again.

For life begs to be lived...
  and the flowers always bend
                toward the sun.

can you see me? can you hear me

Gentle Moments... *all about love*

Love is a resting place.
Marbled, worn smooth by seamless lives, it provides a place to pause,
a place to release the heaviness.

Trees of another time, stand solidly, their
glossy ever-greenery forming
a kaleidoscopic canopy, cradling, rocking...
lifting up.

Love stretches to touch, infusing the spirit, whispering yes
to our dreams.

Here, time and its patterned ticking are silenced, letting moments
for you and me
slide quietly together.

Breaths mingle with the warm air that holds us close.
Love wants to understand.
Love has time to try.

A sharing of the undivided self — eyes, ears, hand and heart,
are given together as one.
Love introduces us to ourselves, when we are introduced to Love.

Gentle moments of specialness — all about Love.

THE INDOMITABLE HUMAN SPIRIT

The human spirit survives. It has struggled to breathe — to be heard — to exist. It will always struggle upward toward the air, it will find its way to the top. There will be shame and many faces of fear and resentment attempting to cover, remove and extinguish, but the human spirit will not die. It flickers even in the darkest of moments.

It is multifaceted,
multi-reaching.
It connects and lifts us
above the base.
It is the part of us that
makes us whole... that
weaves us as one.
Its banner is carried
by the brave.

The human spirit
whispers thunderou
It lingers as long a
there is human life
It must — it is the p
of us that transcenc
and uplifts.

Human Spirit

that which transforms and transcends us
beyond our basic human condition into
that of our human possibility.

It is the part that
earches for answers,
hat will not rest until
it is time to rest,
that will never not
get back up
after a fall.

The human spirit is the
banner of hope that
each of us must carry.
We must protect
and lift it high
and in so doing,
we are uplifted.

It nurtures the love of
spirit, of self and of
others. It rises up
out of our depths,
easing shame
and fear.

It will not die.
It struggles to
survive in
each of us.

It yearns to be heard.
It begs to be known.
It is the catalyst for
the living. It is the
spark for the fire.

This is what I paint — the indomitable spirit of us.

— Karen Holt

can you see me? can you hear me

HEARTBEATS... *of a father and son*

Heartbeats.
Vital.
Pulsating.
Ordered.
Uniquely descriptive of our innermost selves.
One song, and then another.
The distinctive variations dance — diverging and merging,
Blending, flowing parallel to the other.
The interwoven, singular rhythms are shared.
There is deep communication.

This relationship,
a feeling of reverence toward another,
transforms notes into chords,
unifying the melody, creating
a soft, simple song of comfort,
cradled by a love that breathes.

Father and son,
gently holding, wrapping, encircling.
Drawn together, yet with unfettered freedom to move.
Trust is born.

With a hush, a pause, a quietness envelopes.
Clear notes comingle in the fresh air of newness,
imprinting hope into our hearts.

c a n y o u s e e m e ? c a n y o u h e a r m e

Time Together

… without others we lack a part of ourselves

Integral to life is other life.
Essential for completeness is another.

Aged stone, wizened and worn by time — standing, sitting,
each next to another.
Intricately patterned, woven together,
taking time to find wholeness.

Stepping out into the sunshine, watching the shadows move aside,
interlocking,
connecting,
building enduring trust.

Gifts...
gratefully, accepted.

o you know me? can you see m
Karen Holt 1996 ©

REMINDING US...
of our children

They are our children.
They entrusted their hearts.
With hands opened, they came to us
to be held, nurtured and loved.

Crystalline innocence at four years of life,
a wondrous age, bursting with hope,
and we promise to remember.

Children of imagination, curiosity, expectations
and possibilities,

and those eyes — they are like wells of sunshine,
reminding us... of our children.

can you see me? can you hear me

Four paintings, each child at four years of age, each a brother to the next. Each portrait vibrates with individuality. It is not their likeness or similarity in clothing that is intriguing, but rather it is their *uniqueness*, that part that affirms our specialness, seeing past the exteriors of life and into the soul.

TPRINTS… *anew*

A wash of warmness illuminates,
spilling light upon the graduated forms.

Steps created to be often climbed,
a beckoning invitation is offered.
Footprints of humanity imprint their signature,
tracing the steady march of life and time.

Traveling upon a design that lifts and elevates,
each step is interconnected, one not existing without the other.

Standing purposefully together,
the advancing succession is dependent upon those before it,
the finality of one becoming the genesis for the next.

The rhythmic arrangement carries us forward.
Our heaviness finds release in the movement,
and again and again...

We meet ourselves anew.

o you know me? can you see me?

Sharing

... our song

Friends.

Sharing at a soul level,
  reacting with our hearts,
    connecting with humanity,
joining.

A grandiose scheme of interaction and reaction,
  a gift of each to the other.

A warmness within, a heart more complete.
Understanding enough to sing with, to walk with, to fly,
  and to fall with.

Friendship permeates walls of aloneness, breaking down the cold winds.
Well-spent is time when shared with another,

Sing with,
  and we nourish our souls.

o you know me? can you see me?

can you see me? can you hear me

WAITING... *someone is*

Know that there are flowers.
There are paths of jewel-stoned steps,
stretching a myriad of directions.
And there are breezes wafting through
the multi-colored blossoms of all life.

Simple gifts, offered freely,
patiently waiting for our acceptance.

They are reminders that we are not alone,
that we are not singular.
There will always be a light glowing in the window,
a softly cupped hand that holds us — gently.

This hand harbors no ultimatums,
restrictions, or conditions,
only an offering
of a freedom to be.

Always there.
Immovable.
Waiting.

Serenity fills the soul.

c a n   y o u   s e e   m e ?   c a n   y o u   h e a r   m e

TODAY… *is good*

Today is good.
The winds whip at the window.
The chill slips under the door.
But I am strong.
I am filled with courage.
Hope walks nearby.

I pause to see clearly now, as I look into me.
I know warmth,
and today… is good.

TRUST... *the nourishment of the soul*

Vital.
It is like fresh cut grass and the warming sun.
Timeless winds of the earth wrap around us, drawing us together.
As it reaches out and touches, it moves us past our fears and beyond today.
It encourages us to know ourselves.
It beckons us to know another.

It challenges us to hear our own voice and then,
to speak.

It is the clearing, the well worn path,
the constant friend of all — one who sees with his heart.

It is sincere.
It is safe, breathing strength into our being.
It is silent, and yet vibrating with the awakening sounds of life.

Trust — it is the gift that nourishes the soul.
To accept it
brings us home to our hearts.

Best Friends

. . . each to the other

Space around us, so much space,
Movement surrounds us, all around us.
And yet, it seems so still, here inside me.

I am at peace.
You are close by.

Our connection is our very existence,
the breath of each, a gift to the other.

Life is an Adventure

... worth exploring

Grateful.
Cleansed by the wind.
Renewed by the sun.
Its warmth filters through clouds and trees, spilling finally onto you.

The motion — simply round and round and round,
one foot, and then the other, melds with the two-wheeled machine,
falling into its circular pattern.
Changing the scenery, moving towards unknown adventure,
never sure of the direction — spontaneity guides you now,
just moving and trusting, trusting and moving.
Relax, glide, push, climb, reach,
and then fly.

The leaves swirl down and around, some crackling under the whirring wheels.
Startled squirrels catch glimpses as you pedal past, meeting the winds,
creating some of your own.

Hello to the hill — anxiously greeting the climb, and then swooping downward,
its challenge fills the body with confidence, infusing the soul,
lifting the day's weight, with only the truth of you remaining,
bare bones covered in muscle,
a steady, beating heart,
lungs moving in and out,
cares moving out and out and out,
leaving the certainty of you — wonderful you — the gift of you.

Trust that it was meant to feel this way.

o you know me? can you se

you see me? can you hear me

MOVING FREELY... *beyond*

A window of time
looking out
looking in
looking past and beyond
into places and times and spaces unknown
tomorrows yet to live

In and out — away
flying freely
free to see
free to breathe

Free.

Lightning Bug Lanterns

... of love

In the midst of aloneness
I am reminded, I am not.

Melancholy moments lighten, transforming
into delightful discoveries,
as we open to the gifts that surround.

Lanterns of love, carried by firefly-winged messengers,
fluttering lamps, flickering, floating,
rising,
dropping into focus,
moving quickly up and then, unexpectedly, back again.
Flying, winking in the twilight of night —
reassure, remind, renew.

Tinkerbell-like couriers of love — magical and whimsical,
energized by the threads that weave us as one,
restore our spirits,
tickling our hearts into a smile.

And, once again, I am lovingly reminded of love.

o you know me? can you see me?

trust

But Always, Always a Friend

… the constant of love

And as our eyes turn towards
  the wondrous unknown
and all the gifts it holds for each
  unique life,
we are assured that we do not go into it
  alone.

There is a friend,
  be it young or old,
    child or adult,
      father or son or brother,
there is always a friend —
someone to share our discoveries,
  our concerns, our touch, our trust,
    our love,
to walk with, and other
  times to diverge from,

but always, always a friend!

can you see me? can you hear me

do you know me? can you see me?

Gratitudes

I am indebted to many for their invaluable contributions to this project. Those I have known and those I am yet to know, are the reason this book exists. Within these pages, I attempt to acknowledge just a few of those individuals who have shared both their time and their hearts in bringing this book to reality.

This endeavor owes its life in large part to Viola G. Wolsey. My mother's ever present love has given me the springboard of courage I have relied upon when diving into the vast unknown. Her love of life, art, and music infused my soul at an early age, and she has shared with me her determination and strength of spirit, throwing open wide the windows of hope and possibility.

My daughter, my constant, a woman of character, conviction and a heart as big as the sun, the one who has traveled with me through uncharted and often whitecapped waters, has been painted into my canvas multiple times. Her face has often mirrored my own internal struggles and moments of "aha" discoveries. Possessing an abiding power to understand and fully share the moment, she reminds me that if you have something to say today, don't wait — say it now, for you will most certainly have something else to say in the tomorrows that lie ahead. Thank you, Bronwyn Ashley Cole.

My heartfelt thanks are due to Glenna Holloway, poet and journalist, who helped me see the power and the beauty of words, and to Tina Cauller, artist and designer, whose impassioned belief in the project is evidenced and artistically expressed upon each page of this book.

A woman of spirit and passion, Mary Ensor has been a driving force behind this project. She fueled the embers and provided the catalyst to begin my book, again. Her dedication to help victims of domestic violence and abuse is overflowing and contagious. I am grateful she is in my life.

To the lady who walks with me, sharing the sunsets, the laughter, the flowers and the memories, my cheerleader, my sister, Betty Ann Hood — thank you.

And then there are the artists of life — some move the brush or pen, others create the music, but each of you are exceptional in the artistry of living. You have helped me move out from behind the veils and discover my own human spirit. I will not list all your names, for you know who your are. But I am especially indebted to the late Dick Turner, Julia Oehmke, Jeannette LaFontaine, Gary Irving, Frank Karwatowicz, John Harvard, Norm Wells, Rod Keith, Rick Wilson, Lee & Sam Waters, Elaine Schneider, and Jan & Randy Antonson. My life is indescribably different and richer because of you.

I am forever grateful to the Spirit people I have known, those individuals who walk so closely with God that their life and their love light the way for others. Henrietta Smith, Pat Karwatowicz, Rita Harvard, Kathy Casselman Wells, and Rita Dianni Kaleel have been my beacons.

And finally, I am overwhelmed with the energy and dedication given to this project by my partner in life, and the wellspring of my joy, my husband, Ron Isaacson. He is the one who reached out his hand, inviting me to share his life and his heart, offering love untethered, leaving space to breathe, to wiggle and to explore. He helped me to head fearlessly into the wind and to remember that life is truly an adventure vibrating with rich potential.

To the many women, men and children who appear in this book: thank you for the opportunity to know you, and to share with others through art that spirit which empowers and enriches human life.

— Karen Holt

The Paintings

15. ***I AM ME & YOU ARE YOU...***
breathe, balance, stretch – find your melody
Oil on canvas 28 x 22 inches
Ravello, Amalfi Coast
Collection of Health Research Institute

17. ***LOOKING DIRECTLY...***
into the eyes of life
Oil on canvas 24 x 12 inches
Ms. Bronwyn Ashley Cole
Collection of Mr. & Mrs. Kennedy Cole

FORGIVING... invites love *(poem)*

18. ***RAGE... released*** *(left)*
Oil on linen 19 x 31 inches

18. ***SWIRLS... of springtime*** *(right)*
Oil on canvas 24 x 30 inches

19. ***EYES... of a child***
Oil on canvas 12 x 16 inches

21. ***A ROSE IS A ROSE IS A ROSE... within***
Oil on linen 34 x 30 inches
Ms. Bronwyn Ashley Cole
Collection of Mr. & Mrs. Kennedy Cole

23. ***DARKNESS IN LIGHT...***
and still we dream
Oil on canvas 30 x 24 inches
After Vesuvius, Herculeneum

25. ***THE POTTER... and the clay***
Oil on canvas 22 x 28 inches
Scavi Pompeii
Collection of Mr. & Mrs. Joseph F. Kindlon

26. ***COMING BACK... greeting yesterday today***
Oil on canvas 25 x 30 inches
Mrs. Christine K. Baughman

28. ***INSEPARABLE COMPANIONS...***
my shadow & I
Oil on canvas 24 x 30 inches
Positano, Amalfi Coast

31. ***TOMORROW...***
Oil on linen 29 x 25 inches
Collection of Mr. & Mrs. Kennedy Cole

THE HEALING OF THE HEART *(essay)*

33. ***ELIN*** *(top)*
Oil on canvas 27 x 20 inches

33. ***ELAINE*** *(middle)*
Oil on canvas 32 x 43 inches
Collection of Dr. & Mrs. Allen Schneider

33. ***RITA*** *(bottom)*
Oil on canvas 28 x 18 inches
Collection of Mr. & Mrs. Joe LeDuc

33. ***CHRISTINE*** *(right)*
Oil on canvas 50 x 20 inches
Collection of Mr. & Mrs. Paul Valenti

34. ***A BOAT... that will carry two***
Oil on canvas 20 x 24 inches
Snowbank Lake at Ely, MN
Dr. H. Ronald Isaacson
Collection of Dr. & Mrs. H. Ronald Isaacson

37. ***LIFE BEFORE YOU...***
each a part of the symphony
Oil on canvas 29 x 35 inches
Scavi Pompeii, Villa de Misteri
Ms. Bronwyn Ashley Cole
Collection of Mr. & Mrs. Kennedy Cole

38. ***AWAKENING***
Oil on canvas 32 x 25 inches
Ms. Heather B. Lowell
Collection of Mr. & Mrs. Randall W. Lowell

40. ***A PLACE TO BE... where fear falls away***
Oil on canvas 24 x 20 inches

42. ***BANJO BREAK... the strings are to be***
strung, the song to be sung
Oil on canvas 30 x 24 inches
Mr. Pete Norman - "Jalapeño Pete"
Mr. Sam Byerly - "Sammy from Miami"

WITH ME... like music of the heart *(poem)*

44. ***Kathryn Olivia Sawyer*** *(left)*
Oil on canvas 33 x 22 inches
Collection of Mr. & Mrs. Mark Sawyer

44. ***Owen Nicholas Sawyer*** *(right)*
Oil on canvas 33 x 22 inches
Collection of Mr. & Mrs. Mark Sawyer

46. ***DAYBREAK... dancing with light***
Oil on canvas 36 x 24 inches

49. ***I... have known him***
Oil on canvas 25 x 36 inches
Mr. Louis William Stern
Collection of Mr. & Mrs. Louis W. Stern

51. ***BAREFOOT YOUTH...***
unraveling, reflecting, & rephrasing
Oil on linen 34 x 28 inches
Mr. Brett A. Hood

52. ***CHRYSALIS... it is time***
Oil on canvas 24 x 18 inches
Collection of Dr. & Mrs. Sam W. Waters

53. ***EMERALD***
Oil on canvas 24 x 17 inches
Collection of Dr. & Mrs. Sam W. Waters

54. ***HOME IS... in a child's heart***
Oil on canvas 33 x 21 inches
Keaton Smith & Trudy
Collection of Ms. Pam Smith & Mr. Tim Smith

57. ***Mr. Joel Edward Champlin***
Oil on canvas 44 x 40 inches
Collection of Mr. & Mrs. Joel Edward Champlin

58. ***FLOWERS BEND... toward the sun***
Oil on canvas 35 x 22 inches
Kelly Ann Nicastro
Collection of Mr. & Mrs. Neil Nicastro

60. *GENTLE MOMENTS... all about love*
Oil on canvas 24 x 36 inches
Michelangelo's Villa San Michelle,
Fiesole, Italy
Collection of Mr. & Mrs. Kennedy Cole

THE INDOMITABLE HUMAN SPIRIT (essay)

62. ***Mr. & Mrs. Michael J. Birck**, detail (row 1)*
Oil on canvas 75 x 41 inches
Collection of Benedictine University

62. ***Mrs. Rhona L. Stern**, detail (row 2, a)*
Oil on canvas 32 x 21 inches
Collection of Mr. & Mrs. Louis W. Stern

62. ***Mrs. Bess Kindlon**, detail (row 2, b)*
Oil on canvas 53 x 32 inches
Collection of Mr. & Mrs. Joseph F. Kindlon

62. ***Mrs. Jan Antonson**, detail (row 3, a)*
Oil on canvas 27 x 15 inches
Collection of Mr. & Mrs. Randall A. Antonson

62. ***Mr. Joseph F. Kindlon**, detail (row 3, b)*
Oil on canvas 38 x 27 inches
Collection of Mr. & Mrs. Joseph F. Kindlon

63. ***Mr. James L. Moser** (row 1, a)*
Oil on canvas 47 x 36 inches
Collection of City of Naperville, IL

63. ***Mrs. Seyan Raulston Hefner**, detail (row 1, b)*
Oil on canvas 65 x 38 inches
Collection of Mr. & Mrs. William J. Hefner, Jr.

63. ***Mr. & Mrs. John Harvard**, detail (row 2, a)*
Oil on canvas 40 x 28 inches
Collection of Mr. & Mrs. John Harvard

63. ***Andrew Lewis** (row 2, b)*
Oil on canvas 27 x 19 inches
Collection of Mr. & Mrs. Kenneth Lewis

63. ***Mrs. Margaret Jane Franzen**, detail (row 2, c)*
Oil on canvas 46 x 32 inches
Collection of Mr. & Mrs. Gayle Franzen

63. ***NATURAL LIGHT**, detail (row 3)*
Mrs. Kelly Champlin
Oil on canvas 38 x 33 inches
Collection of Mr. & Mrs. Joel Edward Champlin

64. *HEARTBEATS... of a father & child*
Oil on canvas 28 x 23 inches
Andrew & Larry Holtz
Collection of Mr. Larry Holtz

67. *TIME TOGETHER...*
without others we lack part of ourselves
Oil on canvas 30 x 24 inches
Pienza of Tuscany

REMINDING US... of our children

68. ***Geoffrey Rice Champlin** (left)*
Oil on canvas 32 x 19 inches

68. ***Robert Joel Champlin** (right)*
Oil on canvas 31 x 19 inches

69. ***Jared English Champlin** (left)*
Oil on canvas 33 x 22 inches

69. ***Keith Edwards Champlin** (right)*
Oil on canvas 32 x 22 inches
Collection of Mr. & Mrs. Joel Edward Champlin

FOOTPRINTS... anew (poem)

71. *THE STEPS... revisited*
Oil on canvas 16 x 20 inches
Settignano, Italy
Collection of Mr. & Mrs. Neil Horan

73. *SHARING... our song*
Oil on canvas 22 x 36 inches
Ravello, Amalfi Coast

74. *WAITING... someone is*
Oil on canvas 24 x 36 inches
The Steps of Positano, Amalfi Coast
Collection of Ms. Betsey Sink

76. *TODAY... is good*
Oil on canvas 46 x 34 inches
Mr. Lawrence J. Pelka
Collection of Mr. & Mrs. Lawrence J. Pelka

78. *TRUST... the nourishment of the soul*
Oil on canvas 46 x 20 inches
Collection of Mr. Richard E.Wilson

80. *BEST FRIENDS*
Oil on canvas 18 x 24 inches
Panzano in Chianti country

83. *LIFE IS AN ADVENTURE...*
worth exploring
Oil on canvas 32 x 24 inches
The Bicycle Shoppe, Shawnee, OK
Collection of Mr. & Mrs. Larry Smith

84. *MOVING FREELY... beyond*
Oil on canvas 24 x 12 inches
Assisi, Italy

87. *LIGHTNING BUG LANTERNS... of love*
Oil on canvas 12 x 16 inches
Ms. Amber Achilles

89. *BUT ALWAYS, ALWAYS A FRIEND...*
the constant of love
Oil on canvas 14 x 18 inches
Geoffrey & Joel E. Champlin
Collection of Mr. Rod Keith

ORIGINAL OIL PAINTINGS
& COMMISSIONED PORTRAIT INQUIRIES:
Ron Isaacson
1.866.672.5474
www.karenholt.com

Afterword

Inside me
there is a place,
a part I have always known, but could not see.

I did not know she was so empty.
I did not know she was so wise.
I could not hear her tearful silence.
I did not know her…

and the dark is not her friend.
— Karen Holt

There was a time when I knew deep despair. I experienced a life filled with fear, apprehension of the unknown, and increasingly debilitating health issues. I had bouts with immunologically-based illnesses, arthritis at age 28 and asthma attacks that were life-threatening. I did not relate this to anything other than bad luck.

I was a person of acknowledged accomplishment. Graduating with Phi Beta Kappa honors in microbiology, I worked as a research scientist for 15 years. I was married, a mother of a beautiful and exciting child, I was involved in many activities and a leader in the community. My mother was a vibrant role model with a love of music, art and life. Her inspiring influence and can-do attitude are, in large part, the reason I am an artist today. I had studied piano seriously and shared that enjoyment with my exceptionally musical and talented brother. But, I also harbored a fear of public speaking that would often paralyze me. And the nightmares, the struggle of the unconscious to move into my consciousness, filled my sleep. There was an underlying belief that all that I accomplished and all that I appeared to be, was not real. I lived in hopeless fear that others would see me as I saw myself — ugly, stupid, and terribly flawed.

When part of my veil was not quite big enough to cover all that I was hiding inside my subconscious, I crashed. At the age of 44, I reached a point where if I had not let the truth out, I would have suffocated. I was jolted into the past while attending an Alanon meeting, a support group for adult children of alcoholics. The evening's topic was the Fourth Step: do a searching and fearless moral inventory of oneself. My apparent and immediate reaction was obvious to a young man in our group. He stepped up to me later, and with a hug, related how he was also afraid to know something in his life. His intuitiveness touched me deeply. Later that evening at home, I stared into the mirror through my tears, searching for what I needed to know. I looked into the mirror and saw my father's eyes looking back. I then knew it was he — it was my father that I was afraid to know.

With pen and paper in hand, I faced the haunting secrets of myself. I sat alone and wrote. I screamed and felt the ugliness and the fears that I had felt as a child of seven, when I had been first sexually molested by my father in the middle of the night; this shameful abuse continued into my teens. It hurt. It really, really hurt to go back, to be there, to relive the humiliation and feelings of abandonment caused by this perverted role of fatherhood. I was compelled to share this with my mother. In fact, I spoke face to face with her on the very day I first relived and remembered the initial abuse which had occurred 37 years earlier. She was shocked and devastated, but I left knowing I was loved, affirmed and supported in the painful journey that lay before me, and that knowledge strengthened me for the onslaught ahead. A part of myself, the child who had not been recognized for 30 years, began to breathe again, claiming her life as an integral part of mine, and fears began to fall away, just as lifeless branches naturally fall from a tree.

With the memories no longer concealed, real changes occurred in my life. Over a period of three years, I gradually ceased to have the same recurring nightmare. I no longer fought off the unknown attacker, no longer woke to my soundless, silent screams. With time, I have moved from that nightmare of being the victim of hollow, silent cries, to one who screams out for HELP. When I began voicing the word STOP, I knew I had begun accepting the responsibility and the gift of my own life. I do not have those nightmares today. I do not have severe arthritis or asthma attacks. I have let the truth come out and am facing it head on. I regret that I am not able to confront my father, for he died decades before, but with years of counseling, invaluable friends and the ever-present love of God in my heart, at 54, I am healthier and more alive than at any other time. I even finished my first triathlon with my daughter a few months ago.

And where does my twin brother fit into my life? Why has he had such a profound effect, inspiring me to continue stepping forward?

He represents that part of myself that I had unknowingly hidden. I could never stop *seeing* his pain or his truth. His struggles and his abuse by our alcoholic father were visible, apparent and undeniable. Just as I, he carried his own secrets, but I could see and hear and feel his suffering much more than I could my own. My heart cried out for him as a child, and we stood together solidly, both as the protectors of each other and the survivors. We understood each other on a deep level. As a young man of 34, he died.

I gently closed the door and walked away from any relationship I had with God. And with that decision, I unknowingly shut off my life. The nightmares increased, the fear of being alone was immense, my health worsened. Divorce ripped almost all the props that were left out from under me, and I crashed. If it had not been for my daughter's life and her love, I might not have had the strength to survive.

But I have come to know that God does not give us more than we can handle. I had reached the bottom of the pit. I was not perfect; I could not hide my imperfections any longer. I did not have the energy; I was facedown and unable to move. And then I began to see God everywhere: in the trees, in the wind, on the bike trail, in the flight of the birds, and the leaps of squirrels and somehow, I started regaining a sense of strength and life. At this same time, I also began to know love — unconditional love. My husband, Ron, gives me something I had never known — a love based on trust, with freedom to breathe and explore. I was now ready to handle the truth. It had always been there; I just was not ready to know it.

Gene, my brother, was my beacon. He had died more than ten years earlier, but his presence was the guiding light on my road of reliving my memories. He and I walked the road side by side, he always leading the way, nudging and encouraging. It was Gene who inspired me to paint, to smile, to write poetry, and to do this book. He helped define my life work and life mission, that being to help others see and to be seen, to hear and to be heard. *CAN YOU SEE ME? An Unveiling of the Human Spirit* was born from the deep longings of my heart. My hope is that it will connect with yours.

— Karen Holt

Life turns.
It stands not still.
The land moves and shifts beneath,
clouds above reshape anew.

The wind whistles through the bent
ever-greenery of time,
and the clock of life rhythmically
sings out its presence.

And in and through and beyond all that is apparent

Love floats free.

— KAREN HOLT

"Paintings are the inside of the artist revealed."
— KAREN HOLT

KAREN HOLT

In her 20 years as an active artist, painter and poet, Karen Holt has achieved national acclaim for her artistic excellence, elected to full signature membership in both Oil Painters of America, and Knickerbocker Society, a status attained by a select few. Her classical paintings, whether portraiture or genre works, are depictions of quiet, unguarded moments of truth. Expression of self can be seen in each painting, every poem. In the face of her own life difficulties, Karen Holt's artwork testifies to the power of the arts to heal, reveal, and unveil our creative and indomitable human spirit.

can you see me? can you hear me? do you kn
know me? can you see me? can you hear me? c
do you know me? can you see me? can you he
hear me? do you know me? can you see me? ca
can you hear me? do you know me? can you se
see me? can you hear me? do you know me? ca
can you see me? can you hear me? do you kn
know me? can you see me? can you hear me? d
do you know me? can you see me? can you he
hear me? do you know me? can you see me? ca
can you hear me? do you know me? can you se
see me? can you hear me? do you know me? ca
can you see me? can you hear me? do you kno
know me? can you see me? can you hear me? do